The Gap

The Gap

Ian Ross

The Gap
first published 2001 by
Scirocco Drama
An imprint of J. Gordon Shillingford Publishing Inc.
© 2001 Ian Ross

Scirocco Drama Series Editor: Glenda MacFarlane
Cover design by Doowah Design Inc.
Author photo by Debra Mosher
Printed and bound in Canada

We acknowledge the financial assistance of the Manitoba Arts Council and
The Canada Council for the Arts for our publishing program.

Canadian Cataloguing in Publication Data

Ross, Ian, 1968-
    The gap

A play.
ISBN 1-896239-74-9

    I. Title.

PS8585.84014G36 2001   C812'.54   C2001-900236-X
PR9199.3.R5982G36 2001

For Allen MacInnis

Ian Ross

Ian Ross was born in McCreary, Manitoba, and spent the first five years of his life in the Métis community of Kinosota before moving to Winnipeg, where he has resided ever since. Ian has been writing plays for more than 10 years, and *fareWel* (Scirocco Drama) marked his first professional mainstage production. That play was also the winner of the 1997 Governor General's Award for Drama. His first children's play, *Baloney!*, about child poverty in Canada, was produced in the spring of 1998 by Manitoba Theatre for Young People; and his second, *The Illustrated History of the Anishnabe*, will premiere in the 2001-2002 season. Ian is also "Joe from Winnipeg" whose humourous commentaries are regularly broadcast on CBC Radio One.

Production Credits

The Gap premiered at Prairie Theatre Exchange in Winnipeg, Manitoba, in February, 2001, with the following cast:

EVAN MacKay .... Levi Aguonie
DAWN Chamberlain .... Anne Ross
CHESTER MacKay .... Herbie Barnes
SAUL MacKay .... Michael Lawrenchuk
VI Chamberlain .... Patricia Hunter
MR. CONNELLY .... Chimo

Directed by Allen MacInnis
Set and Costume design by David Skelton
Lighting design by Alan Brodie
Sound Composer: Greg Lowe
Stage Manager: Matthew R. Bates
Assistant Stage Manager: Tania M. Olson

Act One

Lights up on an odd landscape. It very much resembles a dry riverbed, only magnified. Cracks and gaps create a disjointed mosaic of earth. Several sandbags are present; they form a small "wall" that cuts across the middle of the stage. A well-dressed, middle-aged woman walks on, VI CHAMBERLAIN. In her hand is a leash, attached to a small dog, MR. CONNELLY.

VI: What's the matter with you?

VI seems distracted for a moment. She begins to chew one of her nails. She remembers her dog, bends down and picks him up.

Don't be frightened. The flood won't touch us. It won't.

She looks at MR. CONNELLY's paws. Inspects them, and walks off. A middle-aged Métis man, SAUL MACKAY, and his youngest son, CHESTER MACKAY, enter. SAUL shakes his head and clucks his teeth.

SAUL: Lookit all that water. I ain't seen that much since 1950.

CHESTER: Let's go, Dad.

SAUL: What the hell for?

CHESTER: I feel weird.

SAUL: What do you mean, you feel weird?

CHESTER: I feel weird walkin' around white people's houses and yards. What if they think I'm tryin' to break in?

SAUL: Chester.

CHESTER: What?

SAUL: There's some of their blood in you, you know.

CHESTER: I know, but I don't care about that, I know if I saw some white guys wandering around our house I'd think they were tryin' to break in.

SAUL: What're you gettin' all paranoid about? If white guys were tryin' to break into our house I'd call the cops.

CHESTER: If white guys were tryin' to break into our house they'd be the cops. Coming to arrest us.

SAUL: Quit talkin' stupid. Make yourself useful.

CHESTER: Where's Evan?

SAUL: Never mind Evan. Just start sandbaggin'. Would you look at all that water? Not since 1950. But you know what? Chester. You know what?

CHESTER: What?

SAUL: Some good's gonna come out of this.

            DAWN CHAMBERLAIN enters. She is dressed in stylish, casual clothes and resembles her mother VI. She picks a piece of something off of her shirt. She is somewhat startled by SAUL and CHESTER.

DAWN: Hello?

            CHESTER stops placing sandbags.

SAUL: Hello.

DAWN: Are you volunteers?

CHESTER: No. I'm forced to do this.

SAUL: Chester. Yes. Yes we are. We come to help.

DAWN: Oh...uhh...thank you. But I think we're supposed to wait for an engineer or something.

SAUL: I can help.

DAWN: Oh...uhh...maybe we should wait.

SAUL: Don't worry. I know what I'm doin'.

DAWN: OK.

SAUL: I've been through this kind of disaster before.

DAWN: Disaster? You think this flood will be a disaster?

SAUL: It already is. Don't worry, though. Good will come out of this. You'll see. OK then. Chester. Get to work.

CHESTER: I am working.

SAUL: Well work harder. I'm gonna go get donuts.

SAUL leaves. CHESTER slows down in his work a bit. He is very uncomfortable around DAWN.

DAWN: What should I do?

CHESTER: I don't know.

CHESTER shrugs his shoulders and keeps working.

DAWN: Uhh...thank you.

CHESTER: Do you got a bathroom I can use?

DAWN: Umm...well.

CHESTER: That's OK. Forget it. I understand.

CHESTER leaves in search of a toilet.

DAWN:	They're setting up some porta potties down the street.
VI:	Dawn. Dawn?
DAWN:	I'm right here, Mom. Where have you been?
VI:	We had to go for a long walk. The dog's still irregular. God, this city's nuts. People ripping people off.
DAWN:	People helping people.
VI:	Charging ridiculous prices for those sump pump things. Whatever it is they are.
VI:	So has anyone shown up yet?
DAWN:	A couple of guys.
VI:	Where are they?
DAWN:	Getting donuts and using the washroom.
VI:	Not ours, are they?
DAWN:	No.
VI:	Thank God. That would have been terrible.

VI leaves. DAWN begins to toss sandbags. EVAN MACKAY enters, a smallish, muscular young man dressed in a t-shirt, jeans and wearing well-used work gloves. He seems hesitant, but walks up to DAWN. He has a slight limp. DAWN does not notice him at first.

EVAN:	Can I help?
DAWN:	I'm sorry?
EVAN:	Hi.
DAWN:	Oh hi. Here to help?
EVAN:	Yeah. I ain't never done this before, so…what can I do?

DAWN: I'm not exactly sure. Heave ho, I guess.

EVAN: Heave ho the dairy o.

DAWN: High ho.

EVAN: Hi ho?

DAWN: High ho the dairy o.

EVAN: Oh I always thought it would be "heave ho". I'm not very good with poetry.

DAWN: I'm Dawn.

EVAN: Evan.

DAWN: Well. I guess we should get back to work.

EVAN: Doesn't look like you stopped.

DAWN: Not really.

EVAN: This is pretty wicked shtt- stuff goin' on eh?

DAWN: I know.

EVAN: I ain't never been in a flood before.

DAWN: Me either.

          VI appears with refreshments. She approaches EVAN.

VI: Sir?

EVAN: No thank you.

VI: You sure ?

VI: Dawn?

DAWN: No.

VI: I'm Vi.

EVAN: Evan.

VI: Nice to meet you.

EVAN: Yeah. You too.

VI: My, you're so hardworking.

DAWN: Yes. Very hardworking.

VI: What's with the attitude, Dawn?

DAWN: My attitude? What about your attitude? Relaxing while we're trying to save our house.

VI: I'm under a lot of strain too, you know.

DAWN: Well do something about it.

VI: Not in front of strangers, dear. I'll be in the house.

               VI exits.

DAWN: Goddamnit. Evan.

EVAN: Yeah.

DAWN: Could you stop for a sec?

EVAN: Sure.

DAWN: Ahm, those go over here.

EVAN: Oh. I'm sorry. I didn't know which place they were s'posed to go.

DAWN: That's OK. I'll help you.

               DAWN notices EVAN's limp and is about to say something, but stops. They form a two person "line" and begin to toss sandbags to one another.

EVAN: I hope everything's OK for you and your mom.

DAWN: Thanks.

               They toss more sandbags. EVAN tosses one towards the river.

EVAN: Whoops.

DAWN: I'll get it.

EVAN: No. That's OK. I can get it.

DAWN: No. That's all right. No problem.

             DAWN goes to retrieve the bag and slips. EVAN helps her up.

EVAN: I could've got it.

DAWN: It's all right. I fall all the time.

EVAN: Not me. You learn balance fast with a crummy leg.

DAWN: Oh. Right. I guess so.

EVAN: Just got to watch where you're steppin' eh? Hey. You weren't trying to do me a favour just now were you?

DAWN: No. Well, kinda. I guess I was, but not for the reason you're thinking.

EVAN: What reason is that?

DAWN: Oh uh. Nothing. Thanks.

EVAN: It's OK. It's always been like this.

DAWN: What has?

EVAN: My leg.

DAWN: Oh. Yes. Well

EVAN: It's OK. It's OK. Just an old war wound.

DAWN: Which war?

EVAN: My last relationship. *(EVAN laughs at himself.)* I'm just joking. I've never been in a relationship. Oh well, shut up now, Evan. Too much information.

DAWN: Or not enough.

EVAN: What?

DAWN: Never mind.

> *DAWN tosses him the sandbag. They work some more and finish for the day. DAWN notices a tattoo on EVAN's arm. In blue ink it says, "WYSIWYG'. DAWN chuckles.*

DAWN: Why do you have that on your arm, Evan?

EVAN: Oh. I don't know. My cousin did that to me when I was passed out.

DAWN: He gave you a tattoo?

EVAN: Sure. We used to do that shit all the time. I gave him a makeover once and put a dress on him.

DAWN: Remind me not to get drunk around you.

EVAN: *(Smiles.)* OK. Stupid thing though, wysiw... I never know how I'm supposed to pronounce it. There's no consonants in this word.

DAWN: Vowels. It's not a word. It's an acronym.

EVAN: An acronym. Like the opposite of something?

DAWN: That's an antonym.

EVAN: A what a nym?

DAWN: Never mind.

EVAN: Do you know what this means?

DAWN: Yes.

EVAN: Holy shit. What does it mean?

DAWN: What you see is what you get.

EVAN: That's me.

DAWN: Excuse me?

EVAN: What you see is what you get.

DAWN: Oh. Do I?

EVAN: Uh, OK.

DAWN: How 'bout a coffee? No, too boring. Give me a call.

EVAN: OK. Know what that stands for?

DAWN: Yes. I even know where it comes from.

EVAN: Really?

DAWN: Really.

EVAN: But I bet you don't know where I come from.

DAWN: Is it exotic?

EVAN: Sure. I come from…well, Winnipeg I guess. Well,
               what a day. What a day. It was very nice meeting
               you, Dawn…?

DAWN: Chamberlain.

EVAN: MacKay.

DAWN: Nice meeting you, Evan MacKay.

EVAN: Yeah. Nice meeting me.

DAWN: So how's Thursday for you?

EVAN: Right. Good.

DAWN: All right. Thursday.

EVAN: Is this legal?

DAWN: What?

EVAN: Asking people out on dates while sandbagging.

DAWN: I think so.

EVAN: Here. I'll give you my number. I don't want to embarrass you or anything.

             EVAN removes a pen from his shirt pocket.

DAWN: Embarrass me?

EVAN: Well I'm...we could meet wherever. You know?

DAWN: No.

EVAN: Well I'm—

DAWN: What?

EVAN: Never mind.

DAWN: So?

EVAN: Well...cool. OK.

DAWN: OK.

EVAN: Better yet. Gimme your number.

DAWN: OK.

             EVAN offers his arm. DAWN smiles and writes her number on his forearm. EVAN crosses upstage. Lights up on two areas of the stage, separated by the small "wall" of sandbags created in the previous scene. One area is the middle-class home of DAWN and her mother, VI. It, like its occupants, is stylish. The other area reveals the home of EVAN, his father, SAUL and his younger brother CHESTER. It is not stylish and needs new everything and a good cleaning. Action occurs in both areas simultaneously. SAUL, CHESTER and EVAN are eating dinner and watching TV. CHESTER lifts half his bum off the couch and farts.

EVAN: What are you doing?

CHESTER: *(Laughing.)* What?

EVAN:	Why don't you go do that outside?
CHESTER:	I'm not gonna get up to go fart.
EVAN:	Well don't lift your ass so the rest of us can smell it.
CHESTER:	That helps to relieve the pressure.
EVAN:	Pressure? Are you gonna hit the ceiling if you don't lift your leg?
SAUL:	You boys be quiet. I can't hear the TV. Chester, next time warn us if you're gonna do that.

CHESTER burps.

EVAN:	Nice. If it's not one end it's the other.
CHESTER:	Just relax.
SAUL:	One of you change the channel.
CHESTER:	Just leave it here.
EVAN:	Yeah dad. We won't be able to get the picture back.
CHESTER:	I'm gonna get us cable.
EVAN:	How are you gonna do that?
CHESTER:	I'll just hook us up.
SAUL:	Turn up the news there.
CHESTER:	It's just flood stuff, Dad. I'm sick of flood stuff.
SAUL:	You'll watch the flood stuff and like it. Tomorrow we're goin' out again. All of us got to get out there and help those people sandbag.
CHESTER:	I got to work.
SAUL:	Work your arse. You won't have no work to go to if the city floods. You boys got no idea. In 1950 we had furniture floating in the living room.

EVAN: Here we go. Why'd you have to say anything?

CHESTER: I didn't.

SAUL: Furniture in the living room. My mom's dining room table bobbing around like a...bob.

CHESTER: Why do we got to help? We don't live by the river. It's just the rich white people who live there. What a stupid place to build a city anyways. Us Indians never used to live here. We'd just summer here and then head up to Stonewall. Right?

EVAN: You can't "summer" in Stonewall.

SAUL: Now Chester. I told you before, we can't blame them for not havin' good sense. Even if they're white.

EVAN: We're part white.

CHESTER: Yeah, but not all white.

VI has broken the silence with DAWN.

VI: All right, I'm sorry.

DAWN: Don't apologize to me. Apologize to our volunteers.

VI: I didn't hear them complaining.

DAWN: That's because they're considerate.

VI: Dawn...

DAWN: Vi...

VI: Don't you address me by my name.

DAWN: Where were you?

VI: I told you.

DAWN: Don't you care that we may lose our home?

VI:	Of course I do.
DAWN:	Well I can't do all of this myself. Or should I ask Mr. Connelly?
VI:	Don't be ridiculous. Where is he?
DAWN:	How am I supposed to know?
VI:	Did you give him his medication?
DAWN:	No. He refuses to take it.
VI:	For heaven's sake, Dawn.
DAWN:	If it's so easy, you do it.
VI:	Let's not fight. Anything exciting happen today?
EVAN:	You mean besides the flood?
VI:	Yes. Besides the flood, which I think is just a lot of hype.
DAWN:	Hype? I swear you're insane.
SAUL:	So what was the exciting news?
DAWN:	Well, I got a date.
EVAN:	I got a date.
CHESTER:	You?
EVAN:	Yeah.
VI:	You what ?
SAUL:	That's my boy.
CHESTER:	Man, I knew I should've stayed.
VI:	While you were sandbagging?
EVAN:	No. During a break.
VI:	I can't believe you.

CHESTER: I don't believe it.

SAUL: That's my son. Finally getting a woman.

EVAN: What do you mean finally?

VI: Do you know this person?

DAWN: Yes. I do now.

VI: Who is he?

EVAN: She's real nice.

CHESTER: Is she white?

EVAN: What difference does that make?

SAUL: Chester. You behave yourself

VI: Well. That's very surprising. I hope this young
             man is decent.

DAWN: Of course he's decent. Aren't all volunteers decent?

VI: Well. I hope he has a good family.

             CHESTER burps.

CHESTER: Well bro, I hope you know what you're doing. Oh
             wait, of course you don't. This is your first
             girlfriend. So when do we get to meet her?

             *The light from a television fills a darkening room
             occupied by two people. DAWN and SAUL
             MACKAY. DAWN, dressed to go out, sits on the
             edge of a large red armchair, balancing carefully so
             that she doesn't pierce her bum on one of the springs
             sticking up through the chair's seat. SAUL,
             wearing work pants and a shirt that needs
             changing, rocks back on his chair. Neither speaks,
             the only sound coming from the TV, which is
             playing a rerun of Lassie. DAWN loses her balance
             and almost falls onto the floor. DAWN does her best
             to recover. SAUL notices and is amused.*

CHESTER calls from off stage.

CHESTER: *(Off.)* Dad. Dad. Where's the ass wipe?

SAUL: I don't know. So. Some flood eh?

DAWN: Yes. Yes it is. Thank you for helping.

SAUL: No problem.

DAWN: I appreciate it.

SAUL: You know, this is my third flood in this city, not counting several minor ones that ruined a lot of basement rec rooms. Back in '79 was pretty bad.

DAWN: I think I remember that.

SAUL: Boy, but not 1950. This one seems just as bad as that one, but we didn't have no floodway then.

DAWN: Do you think it'll help?

SAUL: Oh yeah. It'll save the city.

DAWN: I just want it to save my home.

SAUL: It probably will. I hear that's where you met my boy.

DAWN: Yes.

SAUL: So what line did he use on you?

DAWN: Excuse me?

SAUL: You know? To ask you out?

DAWN: No. I asked him out.

SAUL: You did? Really?

DAWN: Mmmhmmm.

SAUL: Well I'll be.

DAWN: No big deal.

SAUL: You wanna change it?

DAWN: This is fine.

SAUL: What is it?

DAWN: Pardon?

SAUL: What is it? This we're watching.

DAWN: I think it's *Lassie*.

SAUL: It's not my regular. I usually watch wrestling. Or else *Wheel of Fortune*. Or flood news. You never know if we need to evacuate.

DAWN: *(Nodding.)* Hmmm.

SAUL: Did you know Native people never used to live around here, 'cause it could flood. Now look at us. We don't know any better. You can change it if you want.

DAWN: No that's all right.

SAUL: No. Go ahead.

DAWN: All right. Do you have the remote?

SAUL: Sec. *(Calling out.)* CHESTER. CHESTER, COME HERE.

             CHESTER emerges. He's wearing a hooded sweatshirt and jeans. As he emerges from the kitchen:

CHESTER: WHAT?

SAUL: Come change the TV.

             CHESTER changes the channel. The picture becomes snowy.

SAUL: Fix the—

CHESTER: I know. I know. I know.

> *CHESTER adjusts the antenna until the image of "The Littlest Hobo" becomes clearer.*

SAUL: Do you want to watch this?

DAWN: Sure.

SAUL: Well I don't. Change it again, my son.

CHESTER: To what?

SAUL: I don't know. Find *Wheel of Fortune*.

> *CHESTER silently obliges and finds a channel with "The Flintstones."*

SAUL: That's good. I like the Simpsons.

CHESTER: That's not *The Simpsons*, it's *The Flintstones*.

> *DAWN readjusts herself and is now sitting somewhat sideways in the big red armchair. CHESTER "clears" the picture and sits on a couch facing the TV.*

SAUL: This is Denny.

DAWN: Dawn.

SAUL: Sorry. Dawn.

DAWN: Hi. Nice to meet you. Finally.

> *She extends her hand. CHESTER takes it and shakes it lightly.*

CHESTER: Hey. You're the sandbag lady, eh?

DAWN: And you're the sandbag guy, eh?

CHESTER: You're a sandbagger?

DAWN: Yes. Well. Just my house. We don't want to lose it.

CHESTER: Do you know if it's a good-paying job?

DAWN: What?

CHESTER: Like how do I get on to that full time?

DAWN: What?

CHESTER: Sandbagging.

DAWN: You just volunteer. Show up. Like the other day.

CHESTER: It's all volunteer? Shit.

SAUL: Chester.

CHESTER: So what line did my brother use on you?

SAUL: Excuse me?

CHESTER: To like, ask you out. Did he ask if you had any Indian in you?

SAUL: Chester.

CHESTER: Sorry Dad. Hmmm. So can I ask you something?

DAWN: Sure.

CHESTER: What are you?

DAWN: What do you mean?

CHESTER: Well, you're white, right?

SAUL: CHESTER.

CHESTER: What?

DAWN: I guess so.

CHESTER: I'm just asking 'cause you look part non-white.

DAWN: I…

SAUL: Chester. That's rude.

CHESTER: But do you got Native in you?

DAWN: Maybe. My family's French, so…probably.

CHESTER: That's why you're so pretty. You're French.

SAUL: Chester. Don't say that.

CHESTER: What?

SAUL: That she's pretty.

CHESTER: But she is pretty.

SAUL: I know, but you're embarrassing her.

DAWN: That's OK.

On the TV, "Fred" comes home and is jumped by "Dino".

SAUL: What is that Dino anyhow?

CHESTER: He's a dog.

SAUL: That doesn't look like a dog. Did cavemen have dogs?

DAWN: Probably. But I always thought Dino was a dinosaur.

SAUL: That's what he looks like, and he's got no hair.

CHESTER: It's a cartoon. Besides cavemen didn't have cars. Or washing machine elephants.

They watch some more.

SAUL: Let's watch that other show. That hobo show. That's a dog for sure.

CHESTER: Let's just watch this.

SAUL: All these shows have dogs in them. Even *The Simpsons*. Their dog's got a funny name.

DAWN: Santa's Little Helper.

SAUL: Yeah. Santa's Little Helper. That's the most realistic dog on TV, the Simpsons' dog. That dog's so stupid. And he chews everything and shits on the floor. That's just like Evan's dog he had when he was small. What was the name of that dog?

CHESTER: PeeWee.

SAUL: PeeWee. But we called him PeePee, 'cause that's all he did. Pissed in the corner all the time. These kids could never look after animals. We went away once and when we got back their pet bird was dead.

CHESTER: That wasn't a pet. That was some stupid starling that Evan brought in the house and put in a cage.

DAWN: Why did he do that?

CHESTER: It was sick or something. He tried to take care of it. But you can't keep wild animals in cages like that. They die.

SAUL: That's not why that bird died. You kids didn't take care of it.

CHESTER: What were we supposed to feed it? We only had old budgie seed.

SAUL: That would've done.

CHESTER: It was a starling. Not a budgie.

SAUL: You got any animals, Denny?

DAWN: I have a dog. He's really my mother's, but he sleeps with me.

CHESTER: What kind of dog is he?

DAWN: A chihuahua.

SAUL: Bless you.

SAUL laughs at his own joke. The front door opens quickly and EVAN enters. He's dressed to go out, but looks somewhat harried.

EVAN:	Hey.
SAUL:	Here's my hard-working boy.
DAWN:	Hi.
EVAN:	Dawn. This is my dad and my brother.
DAWN:	We were introduced.
EVAN:	So let's go.
SAUL:	You just got here.
EVAN:	We're running late.
DAWN:	Come here. Your shirt's untucked.

> *EVAN approaches her and she tucks his shirt in at the side.*

EVAN:	Thanks.
DAWN:	You're welcome.
EVAN:	Shall we?
SAUL:	What's your hurry? Sit down a little bit, Evan.
EVAN:	We're late. 'Cause I'm already late. So, we gotta go.
SAUL:	Where are you guys going?
EVAN:	Out to eat.
DAWN:	We are?
EVAN:	Yeah. Eating and a movie.
CHESTER:	You guys could eat here.
EVAN:	That's OK.
SAUL:	Make sure you bring my boy back early now.
EVAN:	Dad.
DAWN:	Nice meeting you.

SAUL: You too. And I apologize for Chester calling you pretty.

CHESTER: But she is pretty.

EVAN: Guys...

SAUL: Yes. Yes. OK. See you later.

             DAWN and EVAN exit. Lighting change.

             EVAN and DAWN finish off the meals they have been eating.

EVAN: You have a good appetite. I mean...you like to eat.

DAWN: Doesn't everybody?

EVAN: I don't mean that you're fat...I...fuck. Forget it. Sorry.

DAWN: It's OK. I never went out with someone who ate just meat before. What would that be called? An animalarian?

EVAN: Carnivore I think. It's not a disease.

DAWN: I was joking. Are you OK?

EVAN: *(Gulping water.)* Hmm hmm? Why do I seem not OK?

DAWN: Nervous. Haven't you gone out before?

EVAN: Oh wait? Is that what we're doing? Going out?

DAWN: Aren't we?

EVAN: I thought it was dinner and a movie.

DAWN: Would you chill out. We're not married or anything.

EVAN: Yet.

DAWN: Excuse me.

EVAN: Just a joke.

DAWN: So what's with the meat eating?

EVAN: I don't like vegetables.

DAWN: They're good for you.

EVAN: So's exercise. Doesn't mean I wanna do it.

DAWN: Sometimes we have to do things we don't like.

EVAN: Like?

DAWN: Like this flood.

EVAN: Right.

DAWN: I'd rather be spending my time reading. Or sleeping. But I don't quite remember those things anymore.

EVAN: You will.

DAWN: Will I? I don't know, Evan. I find this all quite scary. What if I lose my house?

EVAN: You'll find…

DAWN: Don't tell me I'll find another one.

EVAN: No. I was gonna say, you'll find you'll do what you have to do. Even things you don't like. Like goin' out with me. I'm kidding.

DAWN: No. It's true.

EVAN: What is?

DAWN: I don't like going out with you.

EVAN: What?

DAWN: I'm kidding. You know what is funny though, I think your brother tried to pick me up.

EVAN: What? Oh no. Did he ask you if you had any Indian in you?

                DAWN nods.

EVAN: Why doesn't he just pull down his pants and walk around naked.

DAWN: He did.

                It takes EVAN a second to realize she's joking. They both rise and reach for where they keep their money.

DAWN: I'll get this.

EVAN: No that's OK.

DAWN: I insist.

EVAN: Me too. You might have to pay for a new house.

DAWN: How about a Dutch Dinner?

EVAN: Oh. OK. What's a Dutch Dinner?

DAWN: We both pay for our own.

EVAN: Oh yeah. Dutch. Good idea. It's good to know the Dutch were good for something besides wooden shoes.

DAWN: It's just a saying. I don't think we're really supposed to say "Dutch" anymore.

EVAN: It's offensive?

DAWN: I think it's a diminutive of "deutsch".

EVAN: Germans?

                DAWN nods.

EVAN: You know how I know that?

DAWN: How?

EVAN: *Sergeant Rock* comics. "Achtung". Or "Gott in

himmell". I'm not sure what that last one means though. Achtung is like in that U2 CD, but "Gott in himmell." Hmmm.

DAWN: God in Heaven.

EVAN: Wow. You're smart. You even know what this means. *(Points to his arm.)*

DAWN: No big deal.

EVAN: So that kind of shit goes on all over, eh? That putting people down.

DAWN: I guess so.

EVAN: My dad just about got into this fight with some professor from the U of M because he told him he shouldn't call himself a Saulteaux.

DAWN: A Saulteaux? What's that?

EVAN: It's a type of Indian.

DAWN: Like a tribe?

EVAN: We don't really say tribe anymore.

DAWN: Sorry.

EVAN: That's OK. You didn't know. I mostly hear "nation" now. Anyways, my dad thought this guy was telling him he couldn't call himself an Indian anymore, but he just meant that Saulteaux was a French word for Ojibway, which is what we really are.

DAWN: Really?

EVAN: Well not really. We're half. The other half of us is Scottish. We're Métis. Some people say mechisk, or mechif or something like that I think. But I don't really know for sure. I hate that.

DAWN: You know what I hate?

EVAN: Indians?

DAWN: No. Why do you say that?

EVAN: Just being paranoid I guess.

DAWN: Why would I hate somebody I don't even know?

EVAN: Happens all the time. So who do you hate?

DAWN: No one. What. I hate this flood that's coming.

EVAN: It's just nature. It's the way things happen. Floods. Droughts. Lightning. Whatever.

DAWN: I like nature. I just don't like what it does sometimes.

EVAN: That's when you go with the flow, sort of.

DAWN: Go with the flow?

EVAN: Yeah.

DAWN: So you're Native?

EVAN: Métis.

DAWN: I figured that.

EVAN: Kind of easy hunh?

DAWN: Not really. It doesn't matter to me though. I don't see race.

> They watch a movie in silence. DAWN takes EVAN's hand and puts it on her knee. She weeps a little at the end of the movie. EVAN produces a handkerchief.

DAWN: (She blows her nose.) I don't usually cry at movies.

EVAN: Me neither. (EVAN sticks a finger in the corner of his eye and shows DAWN a tear.) See?

DAWN: Thank you. Go with the flow right?

EVAN: Right.

DAWN: You mind walking home? I swear my car's never done that before.

EVAN: Sure.

DAWN: That's kind of unusual.

EVAN: What is?

DAWN: Carrying a handkerchief.

EVAN: It's for practice.

DAWN: Practice for what?

EVAN: For when I'm an old man. I figure I'll carry one of these all the time. You know, to wipe stuff.

DAWN: Right.

EVAN: Just kidding. It's a habit. From when I pumped gas. You'd be surprised how handy they can be. I had a good time.

DAWN: Me too.

EVAN: I...liked hangin' around with you tonight.

DAWN: Hangin' around?

EVAN: You know what I mean. Hey, I'm sorry about my dad and brother.

DAWN: You're sorry?

EVAN: Well, they're kind of different than me. They're not very...

DAWN: What?

EVAN: I don't know. We don't get company a lot. I'm sorry I was late. I would have got there quicker, but the traffic was the shits. Not that that matters I guess. I was on a bike.

DAWN: It was OK. I can take care of myself. That's not to say I needed to be taken care of. Your family's very nice.

EVAN: Thank you. Did my dad do his Native speech on you?

DAWN: No.

EVAN: That's good. He has this speech where he talks about being really Native and not Métis and all this stuff, like there's something wrong with that. I don't really care. You know what I mean?

DAWN: You're saying ethnicity doesn't matter to you?

EVAN: Something like that.

DAWN: Great. Me neither. I mean, unless it's for some kind of value or belief or something. So...

EVAN: Yeah?

DAWN: Your family did say something to me. Can I ask you...

EVAN: What? What'd they say?

DAWN: They said you had a pet bird once.

EVAN: Chico?

DAWN: Was that her name?

EVAN: They told you that story about him laying an egg?

DAWN: No.

EVAN: I had this bird. Chico. That's what I called him because he kept calling out "Chee-ko". That's what it sounded like to Chester anyhow. So that's what we called him. And then one day he's sticking his butt up in the air and I think he's sick and he's making this noise. "Waaalk" Like that. And I think he's dying, but the next thing you know he's laid an egg.

DAWN: I thought it died.

EVAN: She did eventually, but we had her for like ten years. We still called him Chico, even though we knew she was a he. I mean, he was a she. I never could figure out what the feminine of Chico was. My dad said "Charo," but I kind of doubt it.

DAWN: That was a kind thing you did.

EVAN: What?

DAWN: Your brother said you found her and took care of her. A little starling.

EVAN: Chico was a cockatiel. Starling? Oh, that stupid bird. Yeah, that one died right away.

DAWN: What happened?

EVAN: My older brother didn't know what to feed it, so he gave it some of his pork chop and I guess it choked. We found it when we came home. A big piece of fat sticking out of its throat.

DAWN: That's awful.

EVAN: I guess. I just wrapped him up in toilet paper and threw him in the garbage.

DAWN: You didn't...?

EVAN: What?

DAWN: I was going to say, you didn't bury him, but I guess the garbage was as good a place as any.

EVAN: I haven't taken in any wild animals since then. It's not right. My uncle had a pet wolf once. Only he could go near it. But there's something wrong about keeping wild animals.

DAWN: I guess this is me. Thanks for the meat. And the movie. I had a really nice time.

EVAN: Yeah, me too. It was a good time. A real good time. So I'll give you a call then?

DAWN: Sure. Or I'll see you at my place.

EVAN: What?

DAWN: We're going to need more sandbags.

EVAN: Oh. Yeah. OK. Good night.

DAWN: 'Night.

EVAN: Dawn?

DAWN: Yes?

EVAN: It was a real good time.

            She smiles and goes home. EVAN turns and walks home, his steps light, with a limp.

            EVAN sits on a large couch in DAWN's living room. VI CHAMBERLAIN walks briskly through the living room. She stops long enough to shake EVAN's hand.

VI: Well hello.

EVAN: Hi.

VI: How are you Eric?

EVAN: I'm Evan. Fine. You've got a nice house. Even nicer on the inside.

VI: Thank you. Dawn and I try. She works so hard, my Dawn.

EVAN: Yeah. I can see that.

VI: Where do you work Eric?

EVAN: Oh. Uhm, different places. Wherever I'm needed.

VI: Kind of like contract work?

EVAN: Exactly.

VI: Hmmm. If you'll excuse me, I'm late for my engagement. Dawn? Dawn?

DAWN: *(Off.)* Yes?

VI: Come and entertain our guest.

DAWN: *(Off.)* I'll be right there.

VI: Now, Dawn.

DAWN: *(Off.)* Mr. Connelly won't take his pill, Mother.

VI: Pardon me. Well, mash it up and put it in his food.

DAWN: *(Off.)* I already tried that.

VI: Well then, you'll have to push it down his throat.

DAWN: *(Off.)* Next time get suppositories. I'd rather do that then push it down his throat. He'll bite me.

EVAN: Can I help with this guy?

VI: No that's OK. He's quite temperamental.

           DAWN enters carrying a small dog, MR. CONNELLY. She has a small bottle of pills in one hand. EVAN approaches to pet the dog.

EVAN: Shit, I thought you were talkin' about an uncle or some weird guy you kept in the back room.

DAWN: Careful. He might…

           EVAN pets the dog.

DAWN: Mr. Connelly's kind of weird.

EVAN: Can I see?

EVAN removes the pills from DAWN's hand.

EVAN: You can't rattle these. He probably knows the sound and that freaks him out. Can I take him?

VI: Careful.

DAWN and VI watch as EVAN takes the dog and gently opens his mouth and administers the pill, massaging the dog's throat as the pill goes down.

EVAN: There.

VI: We'll have to hire you as a nurse, Evan. On contract.

EVAN: Some dogs are like kids. Like needles. You just gotta do it. For their own good.

DAWN: You're definitely good for Mr. Connelly.

EVAN: He knew I wasn't afraid. Dogs smell fear, you know.

DAWN: I've heard that.

EVAN: Can I use your bathroom?

VI: No. I'm sorry.

EVAN: Oh. OK.

DAWN: There's something wrong with it. It doesn't flush.

EVAN: Man. What have you guys been using? A slop pail?

DAWN: A what pail?

VI: A slop pail. You know? So you can. Do your business. We only flush when we have to.

EVAN: Oh. Yeah.

VI: I see. Well. I'm off. And Dawn be sure that you take the parking brake off this time.

DAWN: Yes, Mother.

VI:	*(Imitating DAWN's voice.)* Yes, Mother.
	(VI exits.)
DAWN:	Thank you.
EVAN:	No prob.
DAWN:	Do you want to wash your hands?
EVAN:	No I'm OK. I didn't get no spit on me.
DAWN:	You don't know where Mr. Connelly's tongue's been.
EVAN:	I have a pretty good idea. Besides. He doesn't know where my hand's been.
DAWN:	I have to put him in his kennel before we leave.

DAWN puts MR. CONNELLY into a small kennel and closes its cage door.

EVAN:	Isn't that kind of mean? Shouldn't you just tie him up outside or something?
DAWN:	He has a bad habit of misbehaving if we let him run free. Even when we're home we have to keep an eye on him. Besides, I think he likes it in there.
EVAN:	So do you need anymore sandbagging?
DAWN:	Not just yet. They think it should hold, but could we talk about something else?
EVAN:	Sure. So after we eat you want to go to the zoo?
DAWN:	I don't really like zoos, Evan.
EVAN:	Really? I thought you liked animals.
DAWN:	I do. Just not locked up in cages.
EVAN:	Oh well...me neither, but I figure if people don't visit them they'll get lonely. It's mostly just kids that come to the zoo. And I always figure that can

kinda damage you if you only see kids. Like my auntie Deb, that's all she does is look after her kids or else baby-sit for friends and family. And boy is she grouchy. I'm pretty sure that comes from not being around enough people of other ages.

DAWN: I always like being around kids. They make me happy.

EVAN: For a time. Then I figure it's like being in one of those cages. Our zoo's stupid anyhow. It's got things like Prairie dogs. That's got to be one of the dumbest things you could put in a zoo.

DAWN: They're cute.

EVAN: Not if their holes are breaking your cattle's legs. Then you have to flood them out. Catch them with a string around the hole when their head pops out.

DAWN: Oooo.

EVAN: Sorry. So what do you want to do then?

            DAWN approaches EVAN. Puts her arms around her neck and kisses him. EVAN stumbles back and almost falls over.

DAWN: Are you OK?

EVAN: Yeah sure. I just wasn't ready for that. I lost my balance there.

DAWN: Kind of tricky with your leg, hunh?

EVAN: I'll get used to it.

            He grabs DAWN and kisses her.

            Lights up dimly on CHESTER and DAWN. CHESTER is planted on the couch watching the World Wrestling Federation's "Raw War". DAWN is again doing a balancing act on the big red arm chair waiting for EVAN.

CHESTER: So.

DAWN: Yes?

CHESTER: You must like my brother a lot, hunh?

DAWN: I like him.

CHESTER: Yeah, but I mean a lot. 'Cause it's Monday night.

DAWN: I work most weekends and Evan's usually busy.

CHESTER: Yeah. That guy's always running around.

DAWN: Running around?

CHESTER: Never home. Tryin' to make a buck. I'm sorry to get personal. I'm just trying to help my brother. He doesn't...never mind.

DAWN: What?

CHESTER: He doesn't...you know.

DAWN: Go out?

CHESTER: Yeah. Is that what you guys are doing?

DAWN: Well...we're going for coffee.

CHESTER: I could make you guys some.

DAWN: That's all right. I think Evan wants fancy coffee.

CHESTER: Right.

DAWN: Is he always late?

CHESTER: Usually. He works.

DAWN: Where?

CHESTER: Casual.

DAWN: Is that a clothing store?

CHESTER: No. Like casual labour. They'll hire anybody.

DAWN: Oh.

CHESTER: It's hard for him to get a real job on account of his leg.

                They watch TV. Bret Hart comes on and starts talking about how great a country Canada is, working up the crowd in Pittsburgh, where the "Raw War" is taking place.

TV: *(BRET HART:)* "I live in the greatest country in the world. One that keeps its promises."

CHESTER: What fuckin' planet do you live on, buddy? Boy those guys piss me off.

DAWN: Wrestlers?

CHESTER: Yeah. They don't know what they're saying.

DAWN: You look like you could be a wrestler.

CHESTER: I tried it in school, but it was more like rolling around on the floor and stuff. Not like these guys. Jumping off the top ropes and head locks and figure fours and stuff. See that guy there?

DAWN: Which one?

CHESTER: The one with the short hair and the big biceps.

DAWN: They all have big biceps.

CHESTER: That one with the British flag on his ass.

DAWN: Oh yes.

CHESTER: That guy. I saw him get on the Ellice bus once when I was on it. That's when they still had a Gold's gym on St. James. You ever go to Gold's gym?

DAWN: Shapes.

CHESTER: Oh. Anyways, that guy got on the bus and sat right in front of me. Shit, his arms are big. His name's the British Bulldog.

DAWN:	He looks like a bulldog.
CHESTER:	Yeah. He could probably press about four, five hundred pounds. That's the thing I like about the bus.
DAWN:	What's that?
CHESTER:	You never know who you're gonna see on the bus. It could be anybody.
	CHESTER gets up, and goes to get a drink.
CHESTER:	*(Off.)* Do you want anything Dawn?
DAWN:	No I'm OK thanks.
CHESTER:	*(Off.)* Come on Brendon. Go sleep in the basement. Jeez you, gawann..
	CHESTER enters with a two-litre bottle of Pepsi. He chugs some of it and belches.
CHESTER:	'Scuse me. I usually use a glass, but I'm really thirsty. You know who I saw on the bus today?
DAWN:	I have no idea.
CHESTER:	This guy.
DAWN:	A guy.
CHESTER:	Yeah. I don't know who he is or anything. But he did the most disgusting thing I've ever seen. He was sitting there right? And he was picking his nose. He didn't think anybody saw him. And he hooks this big piece of snot on his finger and he pulls on it. And hollee shit, was it ever long. Like about two inches. Kind of clear with the hard part sticking to his finger. The kind you feel coming out of your head. You know?
DAWN:	Not really.
CHESTER:	Anyways. This guy takes this booger and he starts

sort of rolling it between his fingers, like it was a piece of paint. You ever see artists do that with their paint? Like this. *(CHESTER demonstrates with his hands.)*

DAWN: No.

CHESTER: Or else it's like those guys who lay bricks. And they take the mortar and work it between those whatever they're called. Back and forth. Like that. Back and forth. That's what this guy was doing. Except it was snot. I thought that was kind of artistic or something.

DAWN: Oh.

            CHESTER reacts to the television again.

CHESTER: Fuck, I hate white people.

            He realizes DAWN is there.

CHESTER: Uhhh. Not you, Dawn. Just asshole white people.

DAWN: No. That's OK. I understand. I understand completely.

CHESTER: I shouldn't a said that. I'm sorry.

DAWN: No problem.

CHESTER: I don't mind, you know.

DAWN: Mind what?

CHESTER: That you're white.

DAWN: Uhhh…thank you.

CHESTER: No problem.

            EVAN arrives.

EVAN: *(Seeing DAWN.)* Oh hi.

            EVAN awkwardly approaches DAWN and gives her a kiss.

EVAN: *(To CHESTER.)* Who's that in the kitchen?

CHESTER: Brendon.

EVAN: What's he doing here?

CHESTER: He has to go to work in the morning.

EVAN: Well, put him in the bedroom.

CHESTER: I told him to go sleep in the basement. I think he's crashed out 'cause he took a Tylenol. His foot's bugging him again.

EVAN: Didn't he go see the doctor about that?

CHESTER: I don't know.

DAWN: What's wrong with his foot?

EVAN: He dropped a sledgehammer on it.

DAWN: And he hasn't gone to the doctor yet?

EVAN: He can't miss work.

DAWN: Can't he get compensation?

EVAN: Not really.

DAWN: Are you sure? My uncle works for the department of labour...

EVAN: Let's get going.

DAWN: All right. Bye Chester.

They step outside the front door.

EVAN: I apologize for you having to put up with Chester.

DAWN: He's all right.

EVAN: Next time I'll meet you at your place.

DAWN: Why?

EVAN: That way you won't have to put up with my sleeping nephew or my brother.

DAWN: I like them.

EVAN: It's just not…

DAWN: What?

EVAN: Normal.

DAWN: What is?

EVAN moves his head forward slowly and kisses DAWN.

EVAN: Wow.

DAWN kisses EVAN. They try to leave during the following, but end up sitting on EVAN's front steps.

EVAN: So what'd you guys talk about?

DAWN: Evan.

EVAN: What?

DAWN: You're worried about what your brother and I talked about after what we just did?

EVAN: What are you supposed to say after a kiss?

DAWN: I don't know.

EVAN: Thank you?

DAWN: Never mind. We talked about…the bus.

EVAN: What bus?

DAWN: Transit Tom. And wrestling. And…

EVAN: I didn't know you watched wrestling.

DAWN: I don't. It was neat watching Chester yell at the TV, though.

EVAN: Bret Hart must've been on.

DAWN: I think it was the British Bulldog.

EVAN: Yeah that's one of Bret Hart's cronies. They're bad guys now. They used to be good guys. Wrestlers and their fans aren't very fussy. Did he talk about politics?

DAWN: Politics? A wrestler?

EVAN: Like Canada. Did he talk about how great Canada is and stuff?

DAWN: Yeah.

EVAN: That's what pissed Chester off, then. Chester hates politics. Especially when they brag about how great this country is. It's only great for some of us.

DAWN: Like who?

EVAN: Rich people, for one.

DAWN: I wouldn't know. I don't know any rich people.

EVAN: That's the only time I know I'm an Indian.

DAWN: When you watch wrestling?

EVAN: When I look at what we don't have. Like a bed for my nephew. Or whatever.

DAWN: What does that have to do with being Native? Or Métis. That's what you are right?

EVAN: Yeah. But it's 'cause we're poor.

DAWN: You're poor because you're Native?

EVAN: Something like that.

DAWN: Lots of people in this city are poor.

EVAN: Lots of people in this city are Indian.

DAWN: And Ukrainian.

EVAN: Yeah, but they're not poor.

DAWN: Some of them are.

EVAN: Not most of them.

DAWN: I don't quite see your point.

EVAN: I'm just saying…that there are some things that go along with being Native.

DAWN: Like poverty.

EVAN: Yeah.

DAWN: And being drunks.

EVAN: Yeah.

           DAWN pauses.

EVAN: What?

DAWN: I didn't think you'd agree with that.

EVAN: I don't know a Native person alive who hasn't been affected directly in their lives by alcohol.

DAWN: That doesn't mean that all Native people are drunks.

EVAN: A lot of them are.

DAWN: You shouldn't say that.

EVAN: Why not? It's true. I know more Indians who are drunks than are sober. Sober. Me. My dad. My grandparents. About four of my cousins. Now those who use alcohol on a regular basis. Chester. Brendon. The rest of my cousins. Numbering about twenty-five. My friend Jenny. Solomon. Theresa. Daniel. Summer. All her sisters.

DAWN: Yeah but, Evan. So what? And…don't get

offended. But you're sounding pretty self-righteous.

EVAN: No I'm not. Am I?

DAWN: Yes.

> *EVAN thinks for a while.*

EVAN: I just get so angry. I'm sorry.

DAWN: Apologize to them. Not to me.

EVAN: Who?

DAWN: Everyone you just told me was a drunk.

EVAN: But they are drunks.

DAWN: Let's go, OK?

EVAN: All right. May I have another kiss?

> *DAWN kisses him.*

EVAN: Wow. Nice lips.

DAWN: Thank you. You too.

EVAN: You think so? I've only used them for whistling before.

> *MR. CONNELLY can be heard vocally resisting whatever's being done to him. His "yaps" grow into growls and howls. EVAN enters. DAWN flops onto the couch.*

EVAN: What happened to the pills?

DAWN: I thought suppositories would be easier.

EVAN: I'd take my chances on the other end any day. So when does your mom get back?

DAWN: Anytime now.

EVAN: Wanta…?

EVAN moves closer to DAWN.

DAWN: What?

EVAN: Wanta…you know.

DAWN: Not right now.

EVAN: Come on.

DAWN: No. Evan. Stop it.

EVAN gives up and sits back.

EVAN: Got anything to drink?

DAWN: In the fridge.

EVAN: I'm supposed to get it?

DAWN: Why not?

EVAN: I'm the guest.

VI rushes in. She plops four Styrofoam containers on the table and sits down quickly. She distributes the containers as she speaks.

VI: Pardon my language Evan, but fuck, people are assholes. You'd think they'd be more understanding with all this flood business.

DAWN: Mother.

VI: I'm sorry. I'm frustrated. I couldn't find any decent apricots for what I was going to prepare and now it doesn't matter, because Gerry called me and I have to try and close this deal before I leave on the weekend. So supper's rather simple.

DAWN: Hold it. You're going away for the weekend?

VI: Yes. Of course. It was planned weeks ago.

DAWN: Mother. Our house may be gone.

VI: Pfff. You don't like the vegetables, Evan?

EVAN: I prefer meat.

VI: A meat and potatoes kind of man.

EVAN: Just meat actually.

VI: No vegetables?

EVAN: Nope.

VI: You don't eat any at all?

EVAN: Sometimes tomatoes.

DAWN: Those are fruit.

EVAN: Fruit's all right.

VI: Here you go, my baby boy.

DAWN: I can't believe you're doing this.

VI: Are tomatoes fruit? I thought that question was debatable.

EVAN: What makes a fruit a fruit?

VI: I think it has to do with having seeds and growing on trees.

EVAN: So is pumpkin fruit, too?

DAWN: Those grow on vines. Mother, you can't just ignore this.

VI: Grapes grow on vines.

DAWN: Mother.

VI: What?

DAWN: Forget it.

EVAN: It seems fruit are good for making pies. And vegetables for cakes.

VI laughs.

VI: Then I guess a pumpkin is a fruit too.

EVAN: Yeah, eh.

VI laughs again.

VI: You would think people would concern themselves with more pressing matters.

DAWN: Like what, Mother? A flood maybe?

VI: Oh I don't know. History. Are you all done, Mr. Connelly?

EVAN: That's something I always wondered.

VI: Pardon?

EVAN: Why people do that.

VI: Do what?

EVAN: Talk to their pets like they're gonna answer them.

VI: They do answer. They know what you're saying to them.

EVAN: I don't know. Even a really smart dog's like a dumb little kid.

VI: I'd take the dog any day. Would you like a quick drink, Evan?

EVAN: No thank you.

VI: Just a quick one.

EVAN: That's OK.

DAWN: Evan doesn't drink, Mom.

VI: Why not?

EVAN: I used to drink socially, but I made a vow after my brother stabbed my cousin.

There's silence. VI's pager goes off.

VI: Oh well. That's a good thing then. I guess. Excuse me.

VI exits.

DAWN: Chester stabbed your cousin?

EVAN: No big deal. He only got him in the cheek, so nothing was damaged too bad. He's lucky it didn't get his tongue.

DAWN: Were you drinking together?

EVAN: No. I could never really get into that. But after that happened and I was cleaning the blood off the counter I kind of made a promise not to drink anymore.

DAWN: Wow.

VI returns.

EVAN: Sometimes those things happen in the Native community.

DAWN: What things?

EVAN: Bad things. Like fights and stuff. Or deaths. There seem to be lots of those.

VI: Do you work in the Native community, Evan?

EVAN: No.

DAWN: Evan's Métis, Mother.

VI: Really? I thought you were Spanish.

EVAN: My last name's MacKay.

VI: That doesn't mean anything. Look at us. We're francophones named Chamberlain. Métis is another word for halfbreed right?

EVAN: Halfbreed's kinda negative.

VI: Oh. We used to have a Native family living on the
             corner, when we lived in Silver Heights. They had
             a beautiful daughter. About twice Dawn's age. She
             died though. Killed.

DAWN: When was this?

VI: When you were young. You wouldn't remember.

DAWN: Yes I do. They lived in that big white house with
             green trim. You never told me she was killed.

EVAN: What happened?

VI: She was murdered by her boyfriend.

DAWN: You never told me that.

VI: I didn't want to scare you.

DAWN: You could have told me.

VI: There was never a good time.

DAWN: So what happened? Did you talk to her parents?
             How'd you find out?

VI: Judy Martens told me. I didn't talk to her parents. I
             don't know what happened. I read it in the paper. I
             guess I didn't deal with it very well. We moved.

DAWN: That's why we moved?

VI: Part of it. Most of it.

DAWN: So what if something undesirable happens in this
             neighbourhood? We'll pack up and leave again?

VI: No.

EVAN: Nothing like that's gonna happen.

DAWN: You don't know.

EVAN: Sure I do. There's no Indians around here. Just me.

DAWN: I can't believe you. You too. You're such a redneck,
             Evan.

EVAN: You shouldn't judge a man by the colour of his
             neck, Dawn.

             DAWN jumps up and leaves. VI's pager goes off.

VI: Shit. I forgot. You two will be OK? She'll be all
             right. She's been that way since she was a child.
             Sorry it wasn't much of a dinner. We'll do it again.
             Or have lunch.

             *VI grabs her purse and runs out the door. EVAN
             sits on the couch alone and starts picking the meat
             out of everyone's leftovers.*

             *Very dim lights up on EVAN and DAWN. She's
             wrapped in a blanket. They sit in a park and look up
             at the stars as best they can. They then kiss for a long
             time.*

DAWN: How do you feel?

EVAN: Good.

DAWN: Did you like it?

EVAN: Yes. Did you?

DAWN: Yes.

             They kiss again.

EVAN: You know. That's really funny.

DAWN: What?

EVAN: How hard it is for lovers to find a place to do it.

DAWN: Do it?

EVAN: Make love.

DAWN: That's better.

EVAN: It's really hard though, eh?

DAWN: I guess so.

EVAN: I mean. We can't do—make love at your place. My dad's usually home. Or my brother. Hotels are expensive. You get arrested if you get caught at the park.

DAWN: Good thing we didn't get caught.

EVAN: Yeah.

DAWN: I always wanted to do it outside.

EVAN: I always wanted to do it.

DAWN snuggles him.

EVAN: Maybe that's why they invented marriage. So people wouldn't have to worry about finding a place.

DAWN: If one of us had our own place it wouldn't be a problem.

EVAN: Roommates though. Who our age can afford to live alone? Maybe we should find our own apartment.

DAWN: Or make a schedule.

EVAN: Yeah.

DAWN: I was joking. If all you're going to worry about is where and when we do it I won't be happy.

EVAN: Do it?

DAWN: I'm serious.

EVAN: OK. OK. But it's gonna be hard to control myself.

EVAN hugs DAWN and snuggles close to her.

EVAN: I won't tease you any more.

DAWN: I like it. Just not all the time.

EVAN: Sometimes I wish I could turn off the mercury lamps and then we could see all the stars. Instead of only the bright ones. That's so typical. Only the brightest and loudest get noticed in the city.

DAWN: It's perspective. If we were closer to the dimmer stars they'd become the bright ones.

EVAN: Thank you.

DAWN: For what?

EVAN: Reminding me that things can be good.

          They kiss.

EVAN: And I'm sorry about dinner. I was just trying to joke. It was getting way too serious. You should cut your mother some slack.

DAWN: That's all she's had her whole life is slack. She needs to be reminded that she can't say whatever's in her head. Look at her. There's a flood going on and she's going to the lake. How screwed up is that?

EVAN: It's just how she's dealing with it.

DAWN: Well you can't avoid things like this. You have to face them.

EVAN: You really think I'm racist towards my own people?

DAWN: Well sometimes it sounds like it.

EVAN: I'm angry. That's what that is. Anger.

DAWN: Well maybe you should cut your own people some slack.

EVAN:	My people. That's part of the problem. We make ourselves sound different.
DAWN:	Isn't that what you want?
EVAN:	We want to be treated the same as everyone else.
DAWN:	Then how come Native people have special rights?
EVAN:	That's owed us.
DAWN:	Owed you?
EVAN:	For the land that was stolen from us.
DAWN:	So then you are different.
EVAN:	Let's stop, OK. I don't want to fight.
DAWN:	We're not fighting.
EVAN:	It feels like we are.
DAWN:	OK.

They look up for a bit.

EVAN:	We just made love right?
DAWN:	Yes.
EVAN:	So does that mean we're in love?
DAWN:	*(No response.)*
EVAN:	Dawn?
DAWN:	I guess so.
EVAN:	Good.

EVAN kisses her for a long time. He stops and looks at her.

EVAN:	You want to know about my leg.
DAWN:	I don't care about that.

EVAN: I'll tell you.

DAWN: Why do you say that?

EVAN: I felt it. Just now. When I was kissing you. That you want to know. Were wondering.

DAWN: I want to know lots of things about you.

EVAN: My mom used to do that.

DAWN: What?

EVAN: Tell what we were thinking. Scared the shit out of me.

DAWN: Did your mom die?

EVAN: Nah. She just took off. So you know what happened to my leg? It stopped growing.

DAWN: When?

EVAN: When I was younger. The doctor said it just stopped growing. So that's why I walk funny. My one leg's shorter than the other.

DAWN: Does it hurt?

EVAN: Nah. It just makes me stand out. And it keeps me from certain careers. Like policeman. Ballet guy.

DAWN: Oh really.

EVAN: Hmmm. So anyways, that's it.

DAWN: I like your legs.

EVAN: Yeah?

DAWN: Hmm hmm.

EVAN: Are you cold?

DAWN: No.

EVAN: If we stay here a bit longer we'll see the sun behind those houses.

DAWN: That sounds nice. I haven't watched a sunrise since I was small.

EVAN: That's weird. I'd think you'd do it all the time.

DAWN: Why?

EVAN: 'Cause it's your name.

DAWN: I don't really like my name.

EVAN: I do. I even know why you were named that.

DAWN: Oh yeah. Tell me.

EVAN: Well. There's a certain time in the morning, when everything's beautiful. The streets. The garbage cans. Even the dandelions. Everything. And your parents knew this. That's why they you called Dawn.

DAWN: I think it's more because my parents were kind of hippies. But I like your story better. When is that certain time?

EVAN: A few hours more.

             They watch the sky for a bit. CHESTER comes stumbling on, drunk.

CHESTER: Hey.

EVAN: Where were you?

CHESTER: Just...you know...gettin' snapped. Is Dad back from Grandpa's yet?

EVAN: I don't know.

CHESTER: Hey Dawn.

DAWN: Hi.

CHESTER: What are you guys doing?

EVAN: Watching the sunrise.

CHESTER: What for?

EVAN: Something to do.

CHESTER: Oh.

> *CHESTER stumbles away.*

DAWN: Too bad he wasn't a few hours later. Then he would've been beautiful too.

> *Transition to the next day. CHESTER is smoking. SAUL leans back in a wooden chair on the lawn.*

SAUL: So where's Brendon?

CHESTER: Don't know. Haven't seen him for a couple days.

SAUL: Is he still working?

CHESTER: Don't know.

SAUL: That poor kid.

CHESTER: How come you're feeling sorry for him? You never feel sorry for me when I lose a job. You just give me hell.

> *DAWN enters carrying two cups of tea. She gives SAUL a cup and keeps the other for herself. EVAN is pouring himself a tumbler full of pop. When he is done, he tosses the two-litre to CHESTER.*

SAUL: You should know better.

CHESTER: So should he.

EVAN: Stop it, Chest.

SAUL: And when are you going out there sandbagging again? We got to save those poor people's houses.

Especially Dawn's. 'Course you could come and stay with us if you want.

DAWN: Thanks for the offer Mr. McKay, but it'll be OK. So is it just cattle that are dying on the reserve ?

SAUL: Small things, too. Frogs. Birds. But not horses I don't think. They seem to be OK.

DAWN: I love horses.

SAUL: Me too. I ever tell you one of my horse stories?

EVAN: Here we go.

CHESTER: Which one this time? The time you won the triacta or exacta or whatever it was.

SAUL: Shut up you boys. Not a track story. The love story.

DAWN: Love story.

SAUL: You ever drive to Portage, Denny?

DAWN: Yes.

EVAN: Dawn.

DAWN: Shhh. Yes I have.

SAUL: You ever see that big horse they got there?

DAWN: The white one?

SAUL: That's the one. That area's called White Horse Plains now, but before, the Native people used to have dog feasts there.

CHESTER: Dog feasts.

SAUL: Yup. Dog feasts. They're good.

EVAN: What are?

SAUL: Dogs.

EVAN: When have you ever eaten a dog?

SAUL: I haven't. But that's what I'm told.

CHESTER: You're making this up.

SAUL: It's true. Any Indian who is a real Indian would eat some dog meat once in his life.

CHESTER: Would you ever eat a dog, Evan?

EVAN: What for?

CHESTER: I don't know. Just to try it.

DAWN: Natives never ate dogs. That's just a stereotype.

SAUL: Sure we ate dogs. What's wrong with that? It's an animal. We shouldn't judge other cultures. I don't care if Chinese people eat cats.

EVAN: Dad.

SAUL: What?

EVAN: Never mind. Tell us the story.

SAUL: Oh yes. Well a long time ago, before white people were here, there was this beautiful daughter of a chief. And one day she met this young warrior who wanted to take her as his lover. But there was this other warrior who wanted her, too. And now this is where the story is different, but the way I heard it, the daughter and her young man knew about this other guy that was coming for her. And that her father had already promised her to this other guy. So the old woman who looked after the daughter gave them a white horse to run away on. So they took it and that's what they did. Now the other guy gets there and he says "Where is she?" And when he finds out what's happened he takes off over the plain after them with his buddies. And they ride and chase them and soon they catch up to them a little bit. The problem for the couple was the horse being white. Because it was white it stuck out on the prairie. Very easy to see. So the other guy finds them and he runs them down and they fill the young lovers with arrows. But that horse, it got away. And you can still see that horse's ghost sometimes wandering the prairies looking for those lovers that tried to get away.

DAWN: That's beautiful. And sad.

SAUL: That's how I like my stories.

CHESTER: So what happened to the guy that killed them?

SAUL: I don't know.

CHESTER: Did the chief go after him?

SAUL: I don't know.

EVAN: You're missing the point, Chester.

CHESTER: I get it. I'm just wondering what happened to that guy.

SAUL: He probably lived happily ever after.

CHESTER: Prob'ly. That's always the way. Guys like that never have to pay. It's always guys like me, or else innocent people like the lovers who have to pay.

SAUL: That's why it has to be worth it.

             EVAN and DAWN are kissing on the couch. MR. CONNELLY starts barking. He won't quit.

EVAN: Shut up.

DAWN: Quiet Mr. Connelly.

             They resume kissing. The dog keeps barking.

EVAN: What is his problem? Shut up, eh.

DAWN: Don't talk to him like that.

EVAN: Like what?

DAWN: Like he's worthless or something.

EVAN: He's a dog.

DAWN: I know he's a dog but you don't have to treat him
          like one.

EVAN: What?

DAWN: Show some respect.

EVAN: Respect. That's an animal over there.

DAWN: He's a member of our family.

EVAN: Oh yeah. Where'd you get him?

DAWN: The pet store.

EVAN: How much did you pay for him?

DAWN: About two hundred dollars.

EVAN: You always buy members of your family?

DAWN: So what's your point?

EVAN: Look. I'm trying to be intimate with you and that
          stupid animal won't shut up.

DAWN: There you go again. Don't call him that.

EVAN: What?

DAWN: A stupid animal.

EVAN: Well what is he?

DAWN: You're saying it like he's...he's...not worth
          anything.

EVAN: Sorry. I forgot. He's worth two hundred bucks.

DAWN: I think you should go home.

EVAN: What?

DAWN:	Please.
EVAN:	Let's not fight, OK. I'm sorry to you. And Mr. Connelly.
DAWN:	No.
EVAN:	Come on. I don't want to fight.
DAWN:	Why not? You don't want to talk about things that are important?
EVAN:	That dog's not that important.
DAWN:	He is to me.
EVAN:	So what? You like him more than me now?
DAWN:	All I'm asking is that you show some consideration for how I feel. And what I believe.
EVAN:	And what's that?
DAWN:	That animals are good. They never say bad things to you. They don't hurt you. Intentionally. And they're always there when you need them.
EVAN:	And I wouldn't be. Right? Just like every other Indian.
DAWN:	That's not what I'm saying at all. And don't bring race into this.
EVAN:	Why not? That's what this is all about. You'd never see Native people treating a dog like you do.
DAWN:	No. You just eat them.
EVAN:	It's my culture.
DAWN:	It's not your culture. To eat dogs. Just like it's not your culture to hunt buffalo.
EVAN:	It used to be. Till white people took that away from us.

DAWN: Oh. And we took your dog feasts away too right?

EVAN: That's something we still do.

DAWN: You want to eat dog?

EVAN: Maybe. Maybe lots of Native people do, but we're made to feel ashamed about it.

DAWN: I doubt it. And don't make general statements about Native people. There you go sounding like a racist again.

EVAN: I'm not a racist. You are.

DAWN: I am?

EVAN: Yes.

DAWN: What? How?

EVAN: Everybody is.

DAWN: Everybody is not. I don't care what colour people are. Or where they come from.

EVAN: That's not true. You're always asking me about Native stuff.

DAWN: That's because I want to know about you. And. And I don't want to sound like a racist by saying something ignorant.

EVAN: So you admit you're ignorant.

DAWN: About some things.

EVAN: There you go then. You're racist. Racism is ignorance.

DAWN: Racism is a lot of things. And if I'm a racist, you're a racist.

EVAN: I can't be.

DAWN: Why?

EVAN: Because. I'm a minority.

DAWN: You'd better leave. Evan. Now.

EVAN: OK. But let me ask you something.

DAWN: What?

EVAN: If Native people still ate dogs, would you still wanna go out with me?

DAWN: That's a stupid question.

EVAN: It's a fair one. Would you?

DAWN: But Native people don't still eat dogs.

EVAN: Some do. For ceremonies. Some do.

DAWN: You don't.

EVAN: But what if I did?

DAWN: But you don't.

EVAN: You're not answering me. I guess that's an answer.

DAWN: That's ridiculous. That's like saying if white people were still killing Natives would you go out with me.

EVAN: White people are still killing Natives. And I'm still going out with you.

DAWN: I don't want to do this anymore.

EVAN: What?

DAWN: Us. This. It isn't going to work.

EVAN: What? Dawn, I love you.

DAWN: Just go. Just go. Get out of here.

            EVAN is enraged. He leaves.

            The TV is on. Static. SAUL is asleep in his chair.

EVAN enters. He shakes his father awake.

EVAN: Dad…

SAUL: Hmmm.

EVAN: Dad.

SAUL: Brendon?

EVAN: No. It's Evan.

SAUL: Evan? What is it, my son?

EVAN: I need to talk to you.

SAUL: Change the channel, my boy.

EVAN: Dad

SAUL: What?

EVAN: I'm so angry.

SAUL: Why, my son?

EVAN: I think I broke up with my girlfriend.

SAUL: Oh no. What did you do?

EVAN: Nothing. We got in this stupid fight about eating dogs.

SAUL: Eating dogs. Who's eating dogs?

EVAN: No one. That was just what we were…never mind. I feel…sore.

SAUL: All over?

EVAN: All over.

SAUL: And what about you and Dawn?

EVAN: What?

SAUL: All over?

EVAN:　　　I guess so. But I don't even know what I did.

SAUL:　　　That's OK my boy, that's the problem with us men. We either have no clue what we did wrong, or we know exactly what it is we did wrong.

EVAN:　　　I don't know. It's like there's this big…thing between us. Like I love her you know, and I think she loves me, but…

SAUL:　　　Then you have to fight to get her back.

EVAN:　　　I'm too mad at her, though.

SAUL:　　　So that's why you woke me up? To tell me you're mad at her?

EVAN:　　　No. I don't know what to do. What am I supposed to do?

SAUL:　　　You have to figure that out for yourself, my son.

> DAWN knocks frantically on EVAN's front door. CHESTER comes to the door slowly rubbing his eyes, putting on a T-shirt and cinching up the sweats he's wearing.

CHESTER:　Who is it?

DAWN:　　　It's me, Dawn. Open up please.

CHESTER:　Dawn?

DAWN:　　　Yes.

CHESTER:　Dawn?

DAWN:　　　Yes, Chester it's me. Open up.

CHESTER:　Dawn's not here.

DAWN:　　　What?

CHESTER:　Dawn?

DAWN:　　　Yes.

CHESTER: Dawn's not here.

DAWN: Chester this is serious. Open up.

*CHESTER opens the door smiling. He quickly loses
it when he sees DAWN.*

CHESTER: Sorry I was just having some fun there. What's up?

DAWN: Is Evan here?

CHESTER: No. I haven't seen him in a few days.

DAWN: Did he tell you?

CHESTER: What?

DAWN: About us?

CHESTER: No. You guys broke up?

DAWN: Yes.

CHESTER: Oh man. Now I'm worried. Was it bad?

DAWN: Yes. We got in a fight over my dog.

CHESTER: Over your dog?

DAWN: It was more than that. Have you seen him?

CHESTER: Not for a couple days I told you.

DAWN: Not Evan. My dog.

CHESTER: Why would I have seen your dog?

DAWN: Look do you know where he might be?

CHESTER: Who? Evan or your dog?

DAWN: I need to talk to him. And get my dog back.

CHESTER: I don't know. Maybe at the park. Just a sec, I'll go
with you.

DAWN: No. I'll go alone.

Dim lights up on EVAN sitting by a small barbecue pit near the Assiniboine river. A small four-legged animal is roasting on the grill. EVAN pokes the coals once in a while. He pokes the carcass. DAWN rushes in. She slowly realizes that EVAN is eating an animal and starts to hit EVAN.

DAWN: *(With each blow.)* You... How could...you... I hate you.

EVAN: What the hell's the matter with you?

         DAWN takes a step back.

DAWN: BASTARD. I'm gonna have you arrested.

EVAN: You're the one assaulting me.

DAWN: I hate you.

EVAN: Stop it, Dawn. You're scaring me. What's the matter? Hunh? What's the matter?

DAWN: You ate my dog.

EVAN: What?

DAWN: You ate my dog.

EVAN: I didn't eat your dog.

DAWN: I don't believe you.

EVAN: Fuck you. Leave.

DAWN: Why couldn't you just leave him alone, hunh? He didn't do anything to you. He was old. And sick. He would've died soon anyway.

EVAN: I didn't eat your dog, all right. And fuck you for thinking that.

DAWN: Then where's my dog?

EVAN: I don't know. Wait a sec. You think...not only am I eating Mr. Connelly. But that I broke into your house to get him?

DAWN: What the hell am I supposed to think? Hunh?

EVAN: Think whatever bullshit you want.

DAWN: You ask me all these questions about if I'd still go out with you if you ate dogs. And no. No. I wouldn't. I wouldn't go out with you if you ate dogs. Especially my dog.

EVAN: So I'm just another savage to you.

DAWN: You're not just another anything to me Evan.

EVAN: Then what am I.

DAWN: Is that my dog?

EVAN: Typical.

DAWN: I am not typical. I can't believe you think that about me.

EVAN: Why not? Look at what you think about me. This shit just keeps happening, you know. You guys are over on that side of the river with all the nice stuff and we're stuck on this side with all the shit.

DAWN: I live on this side of the river too, you know.

EVAN: Well, maybe you should live on the other side.

DAWN: Maybe you should stop feeling sorry for yourself I'm going home.

        DAWN starts to leave.

EVAN: Wait.

        After a long pause.

DAWN: What?

EVAN: I wish there wasn't so much...between us. You
           know?

DAWN: Not really.

EVAN: Well that's just the way it is right. I don't get you.
           You don't get me. And never the two shall meet.

DAWN: We met. Evan, we met.

           *DAWN leaves. EVAN sits down. He begins to dig
           out a place to bury the carcass.*

           End of Act One.

Act Two

Lights up on DAWN and VI. They're eating dinner. We also see SAUL and CHESTER watching TV, eating chicken. Action occurs in both areas simultaneously. DAWN and VI eat in silence, VI pokes at her food and drops her fork onto her plate.

VI: Well, where is he?

DAWN: Mother. I told you I don't know.

VI: How did he get out?

DAWN: Maybe he jumped on the doorknob with his little mouth and swung back and forth until it opened. Then he opened the drawer on the bureau, took the spare keys and drove himself downtown.

VI: You never could do sarcasm well.

DAWN: And you never could do drama.

VI: Maybe he's still in the house.

DAWN: Maybe someone kidnapped him.

VI: Don't be ridiculous.

DAWN: This whole thing is ridiculous.

DAWN and VI clear the table. CHESTER takes his plate and SAUL's. He exits as lights fade on SAUL. There's a knock at the door of DAWN and VI's. VI answers it.

VI: Yes?

               VI opens the door. CHESTER is standing there.

               Yes?

CHESTER: Uhhh…is Dawn here?

VI: Dawn.

               DAWN gets up.

DAWN: Hi.

CHESTER: Hey.

               All three stand there for a moment.

VI: Dawn?

DAWN: Yes?

VI: Aren't you going to introduce me to your friend?

DAWN: Mom. This is Chester. Chester, this is my mom. Vi.

CHESTER: Hey.

VI: Hey.

CHESTER: So, uhh…Dawn. Can I talk to you?

DAWN: Uhm…sure.

               DAWN and CHESTER step outside.

CHESTER: Nice to meet you, Vi.

VI: Likewise. Chester.

CHESTER: So, I'm sorry I had to bother you at your house.

DAWN: That's OK. You're not bothering me.

CHESTER: That's good. 'Cause… Look. Man that water's pretty high. You sure you don't need more sandbags or anything?

DAWN: I think we're OK. We're under an evacuation order. We have to be ready to go at any time.

CHESTER: Shitty deal. So… You probably know about Evan right?

DAWN: What?

CHESTER: I was wondering if you could help.

DAWN: I don't know.

CHESTER: Hey. I know you guys are having problems or something.

DAWN: Or something.

CHESTER: Yeah well. Can you still help?

DAWN: I don't know.

             CHESTER removes a pack of smokes. He offers DAWN one. She shakes her head no and then takes one. CHESTER smiles. He lights her cigarette first and then his own.

CHESTER: I could tell, you know.

DAWN: Tell what?

CHESTER: That you used to be a smoker.

DAWN: How?

CHESTER: *(Shrugs.)* It's in the eyes.

DAWN: Yeah, well, once you start I guess you never quit.

CHESTER: You always want more.

DAWN: Exactly.

CHESTER: Kind of like going out with one of us.

DAWN: Men?

CHESTER: Indians.

            DAWN smiles. She laughs a little.

DAWN: I don't know about that.

CHESTER: So do you know what you say after you ask a girl if she has any Indian in her?

DAWN: No.

CHESTER: Do you want some? So look. I'm not asking a big favour here. OK?

CHESTER: Do you know where Evan is?

DAWN: No.

CHESTER: Oh. I thought you might.

DAWN: Maybe he went to an old girlfriend's.

            CHESTER looks behind DAWN.

CHESTER: So, is he here?

DAWN: I meant another old girlfriend.

CHESTER: That would be you.

            DAWN takes a long drag and stamps out the cigarette. She then curses softly and picks up the cigarette butt.

CHESTER: So—if you see him. Could you do me a favour?

DAWN: Sure. What would you like me to do?

CHESTER: Talk to him. Thanks for smokin' with me.

DAWN: Thank you for the cigarette.

CHESTER: No prob. *(Starts to leave.)* Just talk to him. OK?

DAWN: I don't know where he is.

CHESTER: You know.

CHESTER leaves. DAWN goes back into the house.
VI is waiting. There is a silence before she speaks.

VI: Who was that?

DAWN: Just Chester.

VI: I remember his name. Who was he?

DAWN: That's Evan's brother.

VI: Oh. What did he want?

DAWN: Nothing really.

VI: Nothing really.

DAWN: Well, he wanted me to talk to Evan.

VI: About what?

DAWN: Mother.

VI: I'm curious.

DAWN: Incessant, I would say.

VI: Well?

DAWN: He just wanted me to talk to him.

VI: Your boyfriend's brother came to our house to tell
          you to talk to your boyfriend.

DAWN: He's not my boyfriend.

VI: He's not? When did this happen?

DAWN: What?

VI: When did you two break up?

DAWN: I don't think we ever got together.

VI: Oh come on, Dawn. Who are you kidding?

DAWN: What do you mean?

VI: You're trying to tell me you weren't going out with
             that young man?

DAWN: Well...I don't think so...maybe...

VI: Do you love him?

DAWN: Mother.

VI: Were you intimate?

DAWN: MOTHER.

VI: Dawn. We're adults. You can tell me.

DAWN: I don't want to.

VI: Well, you just did.

DAWN: Stop it.

VI: Well, maybe it's for the best.

DAWN: *(No response.)*

VI: He was a little strange.

DAWN: No he wasn't.

             VI smiles.

VI: Hmmm.

DAWN: What?

VI: I think...

DAWN: What?

VI: I think you should talk.

DAWN: I was going to.

VI: Good.

             *Lights up on EVAN sitting in the park where he and
             DAWN first made love. DAWN enters. She*

approaches him, very hesitantly. Without seeing her EVAN speaks.

EVAN: Hi.

DAWN: Hi. How'd you know it was me?

EVAN: You can't sneak up on an Indian.

DAWN: Ffff...

She starts to leave.

EVAN: Wait.

DAWN: What?

EVAN: Did you find Mr. Connelly?

DAWN: No.

EVAN: Oh.

DAWN: I'm... Your brother stopped by.

EVAN: Where?

DAWN: My place.

EVAN: What for?

DAWN: He wanted to ask me a favour.

EVAN: Can I ask what?

DAWN: He wanted me to find you. They're worried about you.

EVAN snorts.

DAWN: Well...I guess I found you.

They stand looking at the ground for what seems a long time.

EVAN: I'm sorry.

DAWN: For what?

EVAN: Letting you think I ate your dog. I'll help you find him.

DAWN: I don't understand. How he got out of the house.

EVAN: Maybe he's still in the house.

DAWN: I looked.

EVAN: Maybe...he went off to die.

DAWN: Shut up Evan.

EVAN: I'm sorry, but animals do that sometimes.

DAWN: Oh. And you would know.

EVAN: Yeah. Bears do that all the time.

DAWN: Mr. Connelly's not a bear.

EVAN: I'm just saying, that when it's a bear's time, they go off to be alone. That's why we never find their bones.

                    DAWN looks at him.

DAWN: Why did this happen?

EVAN: What?

DAWN: This. All of this. You and me. My dog. Us.

EVAN: I...never had a girlfriend before.

DAWN: What is that? An excuse?

EVAN: No. It's the truth. I don't know how to do this. How to be with someone.

DAWN: It's no great mystery.

EVAN: Then why do so many people have a hard time staying together? Or even finding someone.

DAWN: Because they make it hard. When it's easy.

EVAN: If it's so damn easy, why aren't we together?

DAWN: What was that?

EVAN: I needed…

DAWN: No, don't tell me.

EVAN: I want to tell you.

DAWN: Not yet. Walk me home.

EVAN: Sure.

> *DAWN extends her hand. EVAN takes it.*

> *Lights up on SAUL, EVAN and CHESTER. They're eating Kraft Dinner and baloney, watching TV.*

SAUL: Change the channel, my boy.

CHESTER: Dad.

EVAN: Just leave it, Dad. We wanna watch this.

SAUL: Where's the little hobo? Is *Wheel of Fortune* on?

EVAN: Later.

SAUL: Oh yeah. Did you boys finish cleaning out that basement?

CHESTER: Yes.

SAUL: You didn't throw out my papers, did you?

EVAN: No.

SAUL: That's good. 'Cause when it floods I don't want my papers getting wet.

CHESTER: It's not gonna flood, Dad.

SAUL: Oh yes it is. Just like 1950. It's already flooding.

They eat.

CHESTER:	So you and Dawn are back together?
EVAN:	I guess so.
SAUL:	I like that one you got there. She's smart.
EVAN:	Yeah.
SAUL:	So when are you gonna invite her over for dinner?
EVAN:	I don't know.
CHESTER:	Ask her to come tomorrow.
EVAN:	She's probably busy.
CHESTER:	So ask her anyways.
SAUL:	I'll make her bone soup. And bannock.
EVAN:	Great. Skin a rabbit while you're at it.
SAUL:	Good idea.
CHESTER:	What's the matter with you?
EVAN:	Nothing.
CHESTER:	You don't think she'll like us.
EVAN:	She likes you.
CHESTER:	What then?
EVAN:	We can't have company.
SAUL:	Sure we can.
EVAN:	Look at this place. We got no dining room table. No chairs. The arm rests are all crusty. We got one TV tray that doesn't work. No good food. And I can't afford to buy any.
CHESTER:	That doesn't matter. She doesn't care.

EVAN:	Well I do.
SAUL:	Evan.
EVAN:	Yeah.
SAUL:	Invite your girlfriend and her parents over for dinner.
EVAN:	Her mom too?
SAUL:	Yes. Does she just got a mom?
EVAN:	Yeah.
SAUL:	Good. Change the channel Chester.

Lights up on EVAN, DAWN and VI having Kraft Dinner. EVAN is the only one eating.

VI:	How is it, Evan?
EVAN:	It's amazing. This is the best Kraft Dinner I've ever had in my whole life.
VI:	I'm glad you like it. It's about all we have left in the house.
EVAN:	Are you not hungry?

VI shakes her head "no".

DAWN:	Evan thinks Mr. Connelly may have gone off to die. Alone.
EVAN:	Dawn. I was just saying that sometimes bears do that. I wasn't saying Mr. Connelly was dead.
VI:	Do you have any pets Evan?
EVAN:	Used to. But they all… *(He swallows.)*
VI:	Hmmm?
EVAN:	Nothing.

DAWN: I'm having dinner with Evan's family tomorrow.

VI: Really?

EVAN: It's my dad's idea.

VI: Not yours.

EVAN: Well. You kind of need to get used to my family. If you ever do.

VI: Dawn tells me you have a wonderful father.

EVAN: He's OK.

VI: And I met your brother. He seems like a very nice young man.

EVAN: (Smiles.) I guess.

VI: I'd like to meet your father sometime.

EVAN: Sure. Well, Uhm, I'm supposed to…

VI: What?

EVAN: I'm…

VI: What is it, Evan?

EVAN: I'm supposed to invite you over for dinner too.

DAWN: Really?

VI: Really. Why were you hesitating?

EVAN: Well our house is…

VI: Under water?

EVAN: Well…

VI: Tell you what. Don't worry about it. We'll have dinner here.

DAWN: What? Are you nuts? We're under an evacuation notice.

EVAN: Great idea.

DAWN: Why are you doing this, Mother?

VI: C'est parfait fantastique.

> *Lights up on SAUL, EVAN and CHESTER standing at the front door of VI and DAWN's house. CHESTER is holding a casserole dish. VI is doing her best to get everything ready for the dinner. They are using paper plates. DAWN is helping.*

VI: Don't put that there.

DAWN: Well, where am I supposed to put it then?

VI: Here.

DAWN: What are these?

VI: Napkin rings.

DAWN: They look like hair clips.

VI: Go in the kitchen if you aren't going to help.

SAUL: Do they got a nice TV here?

EVAN: I don't know.

CHESTER: You haven't seen it?

EVAN: We're eating dinner, not watching TV.

SAUL: How are you supposed to eat dinner without a TV to watch?

EVAN: Dad. Never mind.

CHESTER: Isn't it kind of early in your relationship to be having the two parents for dinner?

EVAN: This wasn't my idea, remember.

CHESTER: Do you know if these guys like deer meat?

CHESTER lifts up a Corning Ware casserole dish.

EVAN: Call it venison.

CHESTER: Venison. What?

EVAN: Just say venison.

VI: Where's the cutlery?

DAWN: Mother, it's packed.

VI looks in a packed box for some cutlery.

VI: Where is that other set?

DAWN: This is gonna be a disaster.

DAWN and VI hear their guests outside the door. They look at each other.

SAUL: Do they got cable?

EVAN: Ssshhh, Dad.

CHESTER: Go ahead and knock, my hands are getting hot from this venison.

EVAN looks for the doorbell, but can't find it. VI opens the door.

VI: Hello.

EVAN: Hi.

CHESTER: Hey.

SAUL: Hello.

VI: Why didn't you knock?

EVAN: I couldn't find the doorbell.

VI: It doesn't work. Come in.

SAUL, CHESTER and EVAN enter. DAWN gives EVAN a kiss. EVAN starts to remove his shoes.

CHESTER and SAUL follow suit after some nudges from EVAN.

DAWN: This is Evan's father. Saul.

SAUL: Pleased to meet you.

VI: How do you do? I'm Vi.

SAUL smiles.

SAUL: I understand you have a nice TV.

VI: Yes. We do.

CHESTER: Nice place. Kind of reminds me of the McPhillips Casino.

EVAN: *(To DAWN.)* I feel like…

DAWN: What?

EVAN: I don't know. Can Indians be hillbillies?

DAWN: Stop it.

VI: Here. Have a seat, Saul.

SAUL: Thank you.

SAUL sits.

SAUL: You have a nice home, Vi.

VI: Thank you.

SAUL: In my language we say "meegwetch".

VI: Mee…gwitch.

EVAN: Here we go. Dad, did you uhm…

SAUL: Did I what?

EVAN: I forget.

DAWN goes into the kitchen and starts bringing in the meal.

EVAN: Dawn's a great cook.

SAUL: That's good. A woman who can cook is a blessing.

                   The phone rings.

VI: Pardon me.

                   VI uses the phone. SAUL watches her adoringly.

EVAN: Dad. Don't say those sexist things.

SAUL: What sexist things?

DAWN: It's OK, Evan.

SAUL: I won't embarrass you, my son.

EVAN: OK.

DAWN: Evan.

EVAN: What?

DAWN: Just relax.

EVAN: Hey. I think my dad likes your mom.

DAWN: Great.

EVAN: What do you mean?

DAWN: Your dad's too nice for my mom.

EVAN: No he's not.

CHESTER: OK. Where do you want the venison?

DAWN: You brought deer?

EVAN: Yeah.

CHESTER: NO.

                   VI hangs up the phone.

VI: Did I hear we're having deer?

CHESTER: No. Venison.

VI: Right. De...

              CHESTER looks at EVAN.

CHESTER: Yeah, deer.

VI: I love it. I haven't had it in forever.

DAWN: Who was that on the phone?

VI: Just the flood people.

CHESTER: You'll like this deer. We butchered him ourselves.

VI: Really?

CHESTER: Yeah. In the basement. He just about knocked Evan
              out with its smelly ass.

SAUL: Chester. We're gonna be eating. Don't talk about
              smelly asses.

CHESTER: Sorry. Can I sit down?

VI: Sure. Sit anywhere. Everyone?

DAWN: What flood people, Mother?

VI: Oh just a silly evacuation alert.

DAWN: What?

VI: Don't become hysterical, Dawn. Enjoy dinner.
              Where will I sit?

SAUL: You can sit here. Beside me.

VI: Mee...wech.

SAUL: Yeah. You speak good Indian.

VI: Really?

SAUL: Yeah. Do you have any Indian in you?

VI: No. I—

EVAN: DAD.

SAUL: What?

EVAN: Don't.

SAUL: Don't what?

EVAN: Say what you were gonna say?

SAUL: What're you talking about?

EVAN: Forget it.

DAWN: Are you OK?

EVAN: Yeah. Yeah. I'm fine. Let's eat the smelly-assed deer.

CHESTER: Let's eat.

                 They start to dish out the food.

CHESTER: This is like the first thanksgiving.

VI: Thank you. And this deer is delicious. Did you make it, Chester?

CHESTER: Yeah. I try hard to make good food.

DAWN: It looks so good.

CHESTER: Thanks.

EVAN: Chester's big on presentation.

CHESTER: Not really.

SAUL: Chester, pass the salt.

CHESTER: You're not supposed to be eating too much salt.

SAUL: This is a special occasion. Oh. I almost forgot. We didn't say grace.

VI smiles. She folds her hands, elbows resting on the table.

SAUL: OK. No peeking now. Meegwetch Manitou. Thank you, Creator, for all that you have given us. And for protecting us from this horrible flood. We ask that you keep this house safe, but if you can't…then that you'll make sure these lovely people have good insurance. Meegwetch. Amen.

EVAN: Dad.

SAUL: What?

EVAN: You can't get flood insurance.

SAUL: Why not?

EVAN: Because. Because. Why can't you?

CHESTER: 'Cause you live by the river. That's like if you live in certain parts of Wirmpeg you can't get house insurance. Or like livin' on the reserve. You can't get insurance there, neither.

VI: Why is that Chester?

CHESTER: 'Cause houses are always gettin' broken into or burned or who knows what. Our cousin once drove his Chrysler through the living room.

VI: Oh my.

CHESTER: He was OK.

EVAN: This is delicious, Dawn.

DAWN: Thank you.

EVAN: It's so tasty.

DAWN: Thanks.

SAUL: You know what else is tasty. I hear.

EVAN: Dad. Uhhh…don't. They just lost their pet.

SAUL: Pet? I was gonna say dragon fruit. Do you guys have fruit for pets?

CHESTER: Hey.

SAUL: What?

CHESTER: Are plants pets? I guess so eh? Just 'cause they don't walk around and lick your face.

SAUL: Or shit in your bed.

CHESTER: That doesn't mean they're not our pets.

VI: We recently lost a member of our family.

SAUL: I'm sorry to hear that, Vi.

VI: Thank you Saul. Mr. Connelly was the sweetest little dog.

CHESTER: Dog? Oh. Well, get another one.

VI: It's not that simple.

CHESTER: Sure it is. That's the best time to get a new member of the family.

DAWN: Why do you say "member of the family"?

CHESTER: 'Cause that's what they are.

DAWN looks at EVAN.

EVAN: Chester, you've never called any of our pets members of the family.

CHESTER: That's 'cause our pets were more like this deer than family members.

DAWN: What do you mean, like wild?

CHESTER: No. Like food.

VI: Pardon.

EVAN: Chester.

CHESTER: *(Laughing.)* Well not literal food, but kind of stupid. Or not respected. You know?

VI: You should always respect animals.

CHESTER: I do. Even the food ones. But if you give it a name you don't eat it.

SAUL: Vi.

VI: Yes?

SAUL: Did you know that long ago, Native people…

EVAN: Dad. DAD.

SAUL: What?

EVAN: I forget.

SAUL: Oh. What was I talking about?

DAWN: Native people.

EVAN: Don't help him.

SAUL: Oh right. Native people. Did you know that long ago, Native people used to marry French people, and that's how the Métis came to be.

VI: Yes I know. Dawn and I are French.

SAUL: I thought so. You have that beauty in you.

VI: Thank you.

SAUL: What's your last name?

VI: Chamberlain.

SAUL: Oh. So you married an Englishman.

VI: No. I think that's a French name, but I did change it.

DAWN: You did?

VI: Yes dear.

DAWN: You never told me this.

VI: You never asked.

DAWN: How was I supposed to know to ask?

VI: Well...

DAWN: So what's our real last name?

After a long pause.

VI: LaBouef.

CHESTER: La what?

DAWN: LaBouef. Our name is LaBouef.

VI: Our name is Chamberlain.

DAWN: Why didn't you tell me this?

CHESTER: Isn't that French for cheese?

DAWN: Shut up, Chester.

CHESTER: *(Laughing.)* All right. Sorry, Dawn.

DAWN: Mother. I...I can't believe you. Why, Mother? Why?

VI: Calm down, young lady.

DAWN: Calm down. No. You. You're the one who creates these situations and then...and then...

DAWN leaves.

EVAN: Dawn.

VI: She's just upset because of Mr. Connelly.

SAUL nods and smiles at VI adoringly.

CHESTER: Maybe she's upset because of you.

EVAN: *(Simultaneously.)* Chester.

SAUL: *(Simultaneously.)* Chester.

            DAWN storms back in.

DAWN: I am upset because I don't seem to be respected enough to be told anything in this house. How am I supposed to react when I find out my name isn't my name? What if your name isn't Vi? It's Shirley. And what if I'm not really Dawn, I'm Holly. Or Ina.

CHESTER: *(Laughing.)* Ina.

DAWN: It's not funny, Chester.

CHESTER: Yes it is.

SAUL: Chester.

VI: Sweetheart, I know you're upset about something, but please calm down.

DAWN: *(Through clenched teeth.)* Don't tell me to calm down.

            CHESTER starts giggling.

EVAN: Chester.

DAWN: I'm glad you find me so amusing.

CHESTER: I'm sorry. I can't help it.

VI: *(Smiling.)* I've heard that Native people have a good sense of humour.

            CHESTER stops laughing.

CHESTER: What's that s'posed to mean?

VI: Pardon?

CHESTER: You think I'm funny?

SAUL: Chester, that's enough.

CHESTER: No. I want to hear this. You think Indians are funny?

VI: Yes I...I do.

CHESTER: What the fuck...man.

EVAN: Chester!

VI: I don't think they're funny per se, I mean funny, in that they have a good sense of humour.

SAUL: OK. Where's the TV?

VI: I'm sorry, Chester, I didn't mean to offend you.

CHESTER: White people never mean to offend us.

EVAN: Chester. Stop it.

SAUL: Hey, you boys. Stop that. They've always fought like this. I never could take them anywhere. We'd go out and they'd always spill their milkshake or get in a fistfight.

DAWN: Hey. HEY. I'm the one in turmoil here.

CHESTER: Stop feeling sorry for yourself. If you were an Indian you'd be used to family surprises. You meet some guy, hello, who are you? Me? Oh. I'm your dad. Or, what do you mean you're not my mom and dad, you're my granny and grandpa? Ohhhh... All kinds of shit like that. Finding out you got a different name is nothing.

DAWN: Yeah, well I'm sorry I'm not Native. It's so much better. I would get free glasses and free money and land and housing and I would be such a better lover.

CHESTER laughs.

CHESTER: That's right. At least I don't think I'm better than other people.

SAUL: Chester. That's enough.

CHESTER: No.

SAUL: CHESTER. That's enough, I said. Right now. Evan. Get away from your brother.

SAUL smiles and continues to eat.

SAUL: Where's the TV?

DAWN: I don't think I'm better than other people.

CHESTER: Yes you do.

CHESTER leaves.

DAWN: Do you think that, Evan?

EVAN: What?

DAWN: That I think I'm better than you somehow.

EVAN: No. I... Of course you don't think that.

DAWN: But what if I do?

VI: That was the flood people. They're telling us we have to leave.

SAUL: OK then. Let's get this table nailed to the wall. Come on Evan, get moving.

VI: It's OK. Leave them. They're only things.

SAUL: You're sure? Cause I got lots of flood experience. I can have these things high and dry. No problem.

VI: Thanks Saul, They'll be fine. Dawn? We have to go, dear.

DAWN: Evan. Stay.

VI: We have to leave, Dawn.

SAUL:	Come on you guys, this is no time to mess around.
DAWN:	I have to talk to Evan.
EVAN:	You guys go ahead. We'll be right there.
	VI and SAUL leave.
DAWN:	Indian, Indian, Indian. You were trying to warn me.
EVAN:	Warn you.
DAWN:	Yes, Warn me. You were trying to tell you were different and I believed that didn't matter.
EVAN:	It doesn't matter.
DAWN:	Yes it does. When you look at me what do you see?
EVAN:	A beautiful woman.
DAWN:	You see a white woman.
EVAN:	That doesn't matter to me.
DAWN:	You know what I see when I look at you?
EVAN:	What?
DAWN:	An Indian man.
EVAN:	That's what I am.
DAWN:	Yes you are.
EVAN:	What's wrong with that.
DAWN:	Nothing. I always thought that I didn't see race. Now I do.
EVAN:	That's OK.
DAWN:	I'm not supposed to. Don't you see what kind of person that makes me?
EVAN:	Human.

DAWN: No. A racist. That makes me a racist.

EVAN: Maybe everyone needs to be a little racist.

DAWN: Evan. Don't you get it? If I see people as different...

EVAN: Difference is good.

DAWN: But seeing it is not. That means I'm a bad person.

EVAN: No. It means you're not blind.

DAWN: No. It means I don't see you as an equal.

EVAN: I don't believe you.

DAWN: Why? Because it hurts?

EVAN: No, because if you believed that you never would have been with me.

DAWN: Maybe I felt sorry for you.

EVAN: Maybe I felt sorry for you.

DAWN: Look at that horrible thing I felt about you. That you ate Mr. Connelly. I thought, yes, you are a savage. And even if it wasn't my dog... Was that a dog you ate?

          Pause.

EVAN: Yes...but there's a reason.

DAWN: I'm sure there is. But eating any dog...

EVAN: I didn't mean to test you. Only myself. I thought if I ate a dog it would make me an Indian. And I'm not telling you this to try and explain my culture to you.

DAWN: You don't have to explain it.

EVAN: No I don't. But I want to. Thing is, it worked. Eating dog showed me that being Native isn't what you do. Or even how you live. I thought I have to be poor. Or drunk. Or all these other things to be an Indian. I just have to be true. To myself.

DAWN: And that's what I'm being. True. I have been lying to myself. And I don't like who I am. And it's not so easy when you realize who you really are, you're not able to go, oh, so I'm not the person I thought I was. OK fine.

EVAN: Let me help you.

DAWN: Why are you trying so hard?

EVAN: Why are giving up so easily?

DAVM: Because I'm hurting. A lot.

EVAN: And I'm not?

DAWN: No. I don't think you are. Not this way.

Pause.

EVAN: You're right. You're right. Cause when you're Native you get used to pain.

DAWN: I don't want to get used to pain.

EVAN: Sometimes you can't get away from it. I can change my name like your mom all the hell I want to, I'm still gonna have to be who I am.

DAWN: And who is that?

EVAN: Right now?

DAWN: Yes.

EVAN: I'm someone who loves you.

DAWN: And I'm someone who thinks she's better than you.

EVAN: Do you think that?

Pause.

DAWN: Maybe.

EVAN: I don't believe it.

DAWN: Denial. That's not good either.

EVAN: I'm not the one in denial, Dawn.

DAWN: Neither am I. For the first time in my life I've come face to face with truth. What if I think I am better than you? What if my whole life I've been believing that I'm open-minded and free of prejudice and a good little Canadian, but when I get really close to it. I see what I really am. Bigoted. Close-minded. Slightly superior.

EVAN: OK.

DAWN: No it's not OK. And what's really scary is that I'm just realizing that I'm like so many other people.

EVAN: You know it's funny. I always heard that when people were in relationships, you had to watch out. Because the person you were with would want to change you. Make you more like them. But you changed me into me. I've never been more myself in all my life than I am with you. You're embarrassed.

DAWN: What?

EVAN: You're embarrassed. You thought you were a certain kind of person, all those things you said, open-minded, good Canadian...but really, you're maybe a little closed-minded, prejudiced.

DAWN: Yes.

EVAN: Maybe that's what most people really are anyways. But if you're embarrassed about that...good.

DAWN: I don't like how you make me feel.

EVAN: That's not true.

DAWN: Yes. Yes it is true. I do not feel good right now.

EVAN: Am I doing that? Or are you?

DAWN: It doesn't matter. Because I don't want to feel this way. Being with someone you care about shouldn't make you feel bad. And right now I do not feel good. You've been through something. You ate a dog and fine. Something happened. Good for you. But it wasn't good for me. I know we've had some good times together, Evan, but I do not...I do not think we can make this work.

EVAN: Look. I don't know how to be complicated about how I feel. Maybe I'll learn that. Maybe one way's better than the other, I don't know. All I feel is you.

DAWN: I don't deserve that.

EVAN: Deserve what?

DAWN: Your love. After what I said about you. I wouldn't forgive that.

EVAN: It's not about forgiving.

DAWN: I'm not worth it.

EVAN: How do you feel about me?

DAWN: I...

EVAN: Dawn.

DAWN: I can't say.

EVAN: I thought you were going to say you love me.

DAWN: Love's not enough.

EVAN: Yes it is. And you know it.

DAWN: No.

EVAN: How do you feel about me?

DAWN: Stop asking me that.

EVAN: Why? Because you don't love me?

           Pause.

EVAN: You don't love me.

DAWN: No. Evan I...

EVAN: What?

DAWN: I can't say it. How I feel about you.

EVAN: Because you don't know?

DAWN: Because...if I let you in...into all of me...I'll be flooded.

EVAN: Some floods can be good.

           Lights out.

           The End